Ouch!

IT HURTS

Don't Despair
JESUS
Is the Answer

ROSA L. BOOKER

CITI OF
BOOKS

CITIOFBOOKS, INC.
3736 Eubank NE Suite A1
Albuquerque, NM 87111-3579
www.citiofbooks.com
  Hotline: 1 (877) 389-2759
  Fax: 1 (505) 930-7244

Ordering Information:
Quantity sales. Special discounts are available on quantity purchases by corporations, associations, and others. For details, contact the publisher at the address above.

Printed in the United States of America.

  ISBN-13:   Softcover   979-8-89391-505-1
                      eBook   979-8-89391-506-8

Library of Congress Control Number: 2025900567

Ouch! It Hurts, Don't Despair—Jesus is the Answer is wonderfully written in everyday, easy to understand vocabulary. We especially like the way the author wrote about the lives and experiences of biblical characters. For example, although the story about Joseph was written many centuries ago, it is still an inspiration and reminder to us to believe the Word of God and to stand for what is right.

Pastor Ollie W. Bolden and Co-Pastor Cynthia Bolden
Petersville Baptist Church
New Canton, VA

Congratulations on your book. Thank you for being a loving inspiration to our family. The spirit and love of the Lord shows in your heart and in your every day walk with God. We love you our dear sister.

Pastor Calvin H. Booker, Sr. and First Lady, Joyce Booker

Contents

Dedication

It is with much love and admiration that I dedicate this book to my remarkable parents, the late J. Winfred Booker and the late Florine S. Booker. I shall forever be grateful to them for their prayers and reverence for the things of God, which were passed down to my siblings and me.

Acknowledgments

First of all, I give all the glory, honor and praises to my Lord and Savior Jesus Christ, Who I believe inspired me to write this book.

I am thankful for the love, support and kindness extended to me, as we journey through the relaunching of my book *"Ouch, It Hurts, Don't Despair, Jesus is the Answer"*. Truly this was a faith journey.

Rosa L. Booker
Author

A Special Thank You To:

Janie F. Booker

Pastor Faith Jones

Mel J and Joyce Johnson

Deacon Bernard and Sheila Booker

Charlene Brown

Minister Cheryl Bolden

Pastor Ollie W. Bolden

Co-Pastor Cynthia Bolden

Rev. Calvin and Joyce Booker

Citi of Books, Inc.

To each of you who purchased this book, thank you! I pray that this book will stir up the gift that God has placed inside of you—and you too, will fulfill your destiny.

Introduction

To quote Romans 3:4, "...let God be true, but every man a liar " We are to stand firm on God's Word at all times and especially when we are faced with adverse situations and our flesh is screaming, "Ouch! It hurts!"

You may think that *Ouch! It Hurts, Don't Despair — Jesus is the Answer* is an odd title for a Christian book, but I believe God dropped this title into my spirit. Christians are not exempt from the tribulations of this world. In fact, Jesus said that in this world we would have tribulation, but to be of good cheer, because He has already overcome the world for us (John 16:33). Isn't that good news? The purpose of this book is to encourage you in the Lord, so that you won't give up in the hard times. Later, we will take a look at the lives of some of our biblical predecessors and see how they persevered through challenging times.

All of us at one time or another have experienced circumstances that were hard to handle. Maybe it was a failed marriage, an illness, the death of a loved one, the loss of a job, incarceration, financial ruin, or maybe something as simple as plans that did not work out. Maybe you made a bad decision that caused grief to someone else or to yourself. No matter the situation, it hurt so badly that all you could utter was, "Ouch! It hurts," as your eyes filled with tears, but with God's grace and mercy you were able to persist through those difficult times.

Life is not easy all of the time, nor does it appear to be fair most of the time. There will be those "Ouch! It hurts" moments in your life when you feel like giving up, but you know deep within that quitting is not an option. A quitter can never fulfill the call that God has placed on his or her life. Think about it. You will experience the hurts of this world, but how you go through them is key. During those hard times, maintain a good attitude, and learn to draw strength from God, who is able to sustain you and to bring you out with the victory. You must make time for God, so that you can hear His small, still voice. Why wait until you are in a battle before you consult the Lord? Why not keep an open heart and a listening ear for Him at all times. God wants to be first in your life. Why not commune with Him on a daily basis? No substitute will do!

We should never allow anything or anyone to become more important to us than our relationship with Jesus, nor should we try to run our lives independently of Him. I think about time wasted when I would attempt to solve my own problems through my own efforts, only to realize how futile it was. Oh, I didn't think that they were in my own efforts, but anything we try to do from full dependency on God is in our own strength. My friend, it is only through Christ Jesus that we can accomplish a task that is pleasing to the Father. When you experience those "Ouch! It hurts" moments, why not rely on Scripture like Philippians 4:13, "I can do all things through Christ which strengthened me." Jesus said in John, 15:5, "I am the vine, ye are the branches: He that abideth in me, and I in him, the same bringeth forth much fruit: for without me ye can do nothing." There is nothing too hard for God. There is no mountain too high for Him, or valley too low. He is everywhere at the same time. What might seem like an insurmountable task to us, is just right for God. Reach out to Jesus by faith—you can depend on Him. I know because I have found Him to be faithful every time. He promised that He would never leave us nor forsake us (Hebrews 13:5).

I am so excited about my relationship with Jesus, and I so desire to see more of His promises manifested in my life—not for selfish gain, but to be a blessing. How can He who sees the depth of your soul do anything else but pour out His never-ending blessings upon you? My friend, worldly things cannot satisfy spiritual desires. They can only be satisfied through Christ Jesus. When the depth of your soul longs to taste and to see that the Lord is good—like John, you just want to rest on Jesus' bosom. So protected, and so loved—as the Savior cradles you in His arms. What peace, what joy, what intimacy with Jesus! What a thrilling and exhilarating life to live—to cast your cares on Him who cares for you (1 Peter 5-7).

My friend, this world is in a state of mass confusion, and sin runs rampant, but Christians can still have peace through Jesus Christ. Satan is actively launching attacks against us in hopes that we would abort our God-given mission. "Ouch! It hurts" is usually our emotional response to these attacks. Our "ouch" may come suddenly, or it may come gradually. No matter when it comes, it is always a discomfort to our flesh or human frailty. True, we are a spirit, we possess a soul, and we live in a physical or natural body (1 Thessalonians 5:23) and our earnest desire is to follow the leading of the Holy Spirit. However, there are times when we miss it, and allow our five senses, which are: to hear, smell, taste, see, and touch, to dictate our behaviors. As we continue to renew our minds with the Word of God, (Romans 12:2) our spirit-man will become the dominate one, and prevail over our flesh, or human strength.

Beloved, you cannot afford to let anything, or anyone, stop you from fulfilling your calling. You have what it takes on the inside of you to fulfill your purpose in this life. Even when situations look bleak as they sometimes do, you must remember that the joy of the Lord is your strength (Nehemiah 8:10)—and to draw from Him. You don't have to live in confusion or allow the hard things in life to discourage you from achieving your goals. In our born-again spirit, we possess love, joy, peace, long suffering, gentleness, goodness, faith, meekness, and temperance (see Galatians 5:22-23). Jesus will help you. You must continue to meditate on God's Word and to give His Word preeminence in your life.

Born-again believers are no longer under the law, but under grace because of Jesus' finished work on the cross. We are to meditate on the precious promises that Jesus has made available to us.

God's Word is what nurtures us and matures us. It changes the way we think. When we change our thinking, we change our behavior and when we change our behavior, we change our lives. As we mediate on God's Word, and apply it on a daily basis, we become stronger in our inner man. "For the bread of God is he which cometh down from heaven, and giveth life unto the world," (John 6:33).

I don't know what you may be going through right now; perhaps you are experiencing an "Ouch! It hurts" season in your life. I want you to know that God loves you so very much right now—right at this present time and forever. You don't have to try to fix yourself up before you seek Him. Truthfully, He is the only one who can fix any of us. He alone can restore our joy and give us peace in the midst of a storm. Our efforts alone are useless.

I cannot tell you how many times I felt like giving up on writing this book. I felt that it was way over my head, and Satan would constantly try to bombard my mind with all kinds of negative thoughts. He would say things like, nobody knows you, who do you think will read your book? I had to rebuke him, and to press on in the strength of the Lord. I knew that God would see me through.

God is a faithful God, and you can count on Him. As He was with the patriarchs of old, so does He honor His covenant with us. His love endures forever. Let's take a look at some of our biblical predecessors and see how they dealt with their "Ouch! It hurts" experiences. Joseph the Dreamer, Apostle Peter, Sisters Martha and Mary, Hannah, Abraham, and Naomi and Ruth— these were the persons that came to mind as I consulted with the Lord on how to write this book.

"For God so loved the world, that he gave his only begotten Son, that whosoever believeth in him should not perish, but have everlasting life," (John 3:16). God, because of His great love for mankind, sent Jesus as our perfect Savior. In the conclusion of this book, we will take a look at Jesus and see how He has made it possible for us to be overcomers and to live victorious lives. My prayer is that you will be strengthened and blessed as you read through the pages of this book. To God be the glory!

Chapter One

Joseph's Extraordinary Journey

This is a story of love and hate. Joseph was loved by his farther, but hated by his half brothers. Let's follow the story for a better understanding of this family. Jacob loved Rachel and for her father, Laban, for seven years to have Rachel as his wife, and they seemed unto Jacob but a few days because of the love he had for her (Genesis 29:20). This is the union into which Joseph was born. His mother died giving birth to Joseph's younger brother, Benjamin.

Genesis 37: 3-4

I encourage you to read the story of Joseph (Genesis Chapters 39-50) before you continue so that you would have a greater illumination into Joseph's life, and a better appreciation of God's goodness in your own life.

Some may say that Joseph came from a dysfunctional family. He was loved by his father, but hated by his brothers. For the purpose of this book, our emphasis is on Joseph, and how God gave him a dream, and the fulfillment of that dream would cause Joseph to go through unimaginable trials and tribulations. His story should encourage all of us—if God brought Joseph out with the victory, He can do the same for us.

Joseph endured much hardship because of his brothers' jealousy; they threw him into a pit and sold him into slavery. That in itself is enough to make anyone say, "Ouch! It hurts." The good news is that Joseph not only survived the pit experience, but Joseph, with God's help went from the pit to the palace. God did it for Joseph, and He wants to raise you out of your pit experience—"God is no respecter of persons (Acts 10:34)." What pit are you in today? Do you have the faith to believe God, and not give up during the hard times? If Joseph could do it under such extreme hardships, so can we. We have a better covenant with God than Joseph had. I believe there is a Joseph persona in each of us. We have the God given desire to want more out of life than the status quo. We have divine purpose and destiny on the inside of us, longing to be unleashed.

Joseph's Dream

At the age of seventeen Joseph dreamed a dream that would revolutionize his life forever. His dream was so powerful that he found it difficult to contain, so he excitedly shared it with his family. It was a dream from God!

"And Joseph dreamed a dream, and he told it his brethren: and they hated him yet the more. And he said unto them, Hear, I pray you, this dream which I have dreamed: For, behold, we were binding sheaves in the field, and, lo, my sheaf arose, and also stood upright; and, behold, your sheaves stood round about, and made obeisance to my sheaf. And his brethren said to him, Shalt thou indeed reign over us? or shalt thou indeed have dominion over us? And they hated him yet the more for his dreams, and for his words. And he dreamed yet another dream, and told it his brethren, and said, Behold, I have dreamed a dream more; and, behold, the sun and the moon and the eleven stars made obeisance to me. And he told it to his father, and to his brethren: and his father rebuked him, and said unto him, What is this dream that thou hast dreamed? Shall I and thy mother and thy brethren indeed come to bow down ourselves to thee to the earth? And his brethren envied him; but his father observed the saying."

Genesis 37:5-11

Joseph's family did not want to hear about his dream. In fact, they resented him for telling it. The Scripture says his father rebuked him and his brothers who already hated him, hated him even more. Can you imagine how Joseph must have felt?

Family is extremely important to us; we value their opinions, and we long for their support. Joseph paid a tremendous price to see his dream realized. He faced many challenges, but the Lord was with Joseph. When he was thrown into the pit, he did not die; when he was sold into slavery, he became a successful man. Whatsoever Joseph put his hands to do, he prospered because God was with Him.

Joseph: A Slave

"AND Joseph was brought down to Egypt; and Potiphar, an officer of Pharaoh, captain of the guard, an Egyptian, bought him of the hands of the Ishmeelites, which had brought him down thither. And the LORD was with Joseph, and he was a prosperous man; and he was in the house of his master the Egyptian. And his master saw that the LORD was with him, and that the LORD made all that he did to prosper in his hand. And Joseph found grace in his sight, and he served him: and he made him overseer over his house, and all that he had he put into his hand."

Genesis 39:1-4

Joseph was a man of integrity—an excellent worker. Potiphar had no need to worry about anything concerning the affairs of his house while Joseph was in charge (Genesis 39). He put Joseph in charge of his entire household with the exception of his wife. Potiphar's wife, however, found Joseph attractive, and she lusted after him day after day, but Joseph's desire was to please God and he would not submit to her evil wishes. As it were, one day when Joseph went into the house as usual to take care of the household affairs, none of the other servants were in the house only Joseph and Potiphar's wife. She made another attempt to seduce Joseph and lunged at him. As he ran away from her, she managed to grab his coat. She was furious that Joseph did not fall prey to her desires, so she lied to her husband that Joseph had tried to make sexual advances towards her. When she showed her husband Joseph's coat as her evidence, he became angry and had Joseph thrown into prison. Hurt and disappointed, an innocent man now found himself incarcerated. Can you envision how deeply this must have hurt Joseph—but God was with Joseph, and he found favor with the warden of the prison. In fact, the warden put all of the other prisoners under Joseph's care.

My friend, this is how God works in our lives. The very thing that the enemy would try to use to destroy us—God, by His grace and mercy will somehow turn that awful situation around and cause it to work for our good (Romans 8:28). What a loving and awesome God we serve!

"But the LORD was with Joseph, and shewed him mercy, and gave him favour in the sight of the keeper of the prison. And the keeper of the prison committed to Joseph's hand all the prisoners that were in the prison; and whatsoever they did there, he was the doer of it. The keeper of the prison looked not to any thing that was under his hand; because the LORD was with him, and that which he did, the LORD made it to prosper."

Genesis 39:21-23

One day Joseph noticed that the countenance of Pharaoh's officers who were in custody with him looked sad. Joseph inquired of them, and they both had dreamed dreams that disturbed them, and there was no one who could interpret their dreams. Joseph let them know that this gift of interpretation belongs to God–then he interpreted their dreams. He told the butler that he would return to his previous position with Pharaoh and told the baker that he would hang at the hands of the Pharaoh. These events occurred just as Joseph had said. Joseph asked the butler to remember him when he was released, but the butler soon forgot about Joseph.

(Genesis 40)

Isn't it amazing how we sometimes forget about those who have helped us along the way—to our "better place?" When circumstances are bad, we have a tendency to make all kinds of promises, but when life is better, those promises are soon forgotten. God is not like that! He always keeps His Word.

From the Prison to the Palace

Some two years later, Pharaoh had a dream, and no one that he knew could interpret his dream. It was not until then that the butler remembered his dream when he was incarcerated. He told Pharaoh that only Joseph could interpret his and the baker's dreams, and it happened just as Joseph had said. Immediately Pharaoh sent for Joseph and they brought him hastily out of prison. Joseph made himself presentable and was brought before Pharaoh. Joseph was able to interpret Pharaoh's dream. Egypt would go through seven years of plenty and seven years of famine. The Lord imparted Godly wisdom unto Joseph, so he was able to share a plan with Pharaoh and his staff that would prepare them for the inevitable. Pharaoh and his servants were well pleased with Joseph's insight, and Pharaoh put Joseph in charge over his house and second in charge of Egypt.

"And Pharaoh said unto his servants, Can we find such a one as this is, a man in whom the Spirit of God is? And Pharaoh said unto Joseph, For as much as God hath shewn thee all this, there is none so discreet and wise as thou art: Thou shalt be over my house, and according unto thy word shall all my people be ruled: only in the throne will I be greater than thou. And Pharaoh said unto Joseph, See, I have set thee over all the land of Egypt. And Pharaoh took off his ring from his hand, and put it upon Joseph's hand, and arrayed

him in vestures of fine linen, and put a gold chain about his neck; And he made him to ride in the second chariot which he had; and they cried before him, Bow the knee: and he made him ruler over all the land of Egypt. And Pharaoh said unto Joseph, I am Pharaoh, and without thee shall no man lift up his hand or foot in all the land of Egypt. "

Genesis 41: 38-44

No Hard Feelings Brothers!

Joseph was a young man when his troubles began. In a sense, it looked as if there was no way out! His brothers' cruel and calculated scheme was hurtful. His abrupt separation from his family—his father, and brother Benjamin, in particular—was a hard place to be. Joseph's father Jacob, believed that Joseph had been killed by a wild beast—when in fact, Joseph's brothers killed a baby goat and dipped Joseph's coat in the blood, and brought Joseph's coat to their father (Genesis 37:31-32). With this apparent evidence, it appeared that Joseph's life was doomed to destruction, but God was with Joseph!

With all that Joseph went through, he refused to succumb to bitterness and hatred. If anyone had a reason to be bitter it would have been Joseph. However, he would not allow the enemy to win. Like Joseph, each of us will encounter trials and tribulations during our earthly lives. We can choose to go through them in the strength of the Lord, or we can take matters into our own hands, and try to fight our own battles. The choice is yours—which will you choose?

No matter how hard life may become, or how many times people may hurt us, we must forgive and keep moving forward with life, and move forward in the Lord. Life is precious, and we only get one chance at it on this earth. Our earthly life is not a "rehearsal," but the real deal to accomplish what God has instructed us to do. We cannot afford to wallow in self-pity, and camp out in hurt feelings. They will poison our future. We must move forward with kingdom living and kingdom work.

As the story continues, Joseph and his brothers met again. His brothers came to Egypt to purchase grain because of the severity of the famine. They bowed down in homage to Joseph because of his position as governor of Egypt, not knowing who he was, but Joseph recognized them immediately.

And Joseph was the governor over the land, and he it was that sold to all the people of the land: and Joseph's brethren came, and bowed down themselves before him with their faces to the earth. And Joseph saw his brethren, and he knew them, but made himself strange unto them, and spake roughly unto them; and he said unto them, Whence come ye? And they said, From the land of Canaan to buy food. And Joseph knew his brethren, but they knew not him. And Joseph remembered the dreams which be dreamed of them, and said unto them, Ye are spies; to see the nakedness of the land ye are come. And they said unto him, Nay, my lord, but to buy food are thy servants come.

Genesis 42:6-10

Although, Joseph recognized his brothers, he did not know how they had made it over the years or how many of them were still alive. He began to question them about their family. When they told him about Benjamin, and his father, he desperately longed to see them. Joseph orchestrated a plan that would have his brothers to bring Benjamin to him, which eventually led to Joseph revealing himself to his brothers.

And Joseph said unto his brethren, Come near to me, I pray you. And they came near. And he said, I am Joseph your brother, whom ye sold into Egypt. Now therefore be not grieved, nor angry with yourselves, that ye sold me hither: for God did send me before you to preserve life.

Genesis 45:4-5

Joseph then sent for his father and his father's household, which numbered seventy in all that came to live in Egypt. Pharaoh provided well for Joseph's family and they lived in abundance.

When Jacob died, Joseph's brothers became frightened of Joseph and what he might do to them. Their own guilty consciences tormented them, and they would not believe that Joseph had indeed forgiven them for the harm that they had caused him.

"And when Joseph's brethren saw that their father was dead, they said, Joseph will peradventure hate us, and will certainly requite us all the evil which we did unto him. And they sent a messenger unto Joseph, saying, Thy father did command before he died, saying, So shall ye say unto Joseph, Forgive, I pray thee now, the trespass of thy brethren, and their sin; for they did unto thee evil: and now, we pray thee, forgive the trespass of the servants of the God of thy father. And Joseph wept when they spake unto him. And his brethren also went and fell down before his face; and they said, Behold, we be thy servants. And Joseph said unto them, Fear not: for am I in the place of God? But as for you, ye thought evil against me; but God meant it unto good, to bring to pass, as it is this day, to save much people alive. Now therefore fear ye not: I will nourish you, and your little ones. And he comforted them, and spake kindly unto them."

Genesis 50:15-21

His brothers had no need to fear retribution. God's goodness on Joseph's life far exceeded any hurt that his brothers had caused him.

When you make up your mind to go after God, He will bring you out with the victory, no matter how impossible your dream may seem or what trials and tribulations you may have to endure.

Has God given you a dream that seems impossible or a calling that seems too hard to do? Do you find yourself putting it off because you feel so insignificant? Do you see yourself with the "grasshopper's mentality?" (Numbers 13:33). Are you waiting for someone else to validate your dream? Friend, if God has given you a dream or a calling, I strongly encourage you to pursue it. He will help you!

To fulfill your dream or calling will take "grit your teeth" determination, much prayer and your obedience to God's instructions. One of the many things that I so admire about the Lord is that He does not give up on us! Like Paul, I too, am encouraged by Philippians 1:6, "Being confident of this very thing, that he which hath begun a good work in you will perform it until the day of Jesus Christ."

Steps to Your Destiny

When I received my assignment to write this book, I thought it was a "right now" project, but it wasn't. Friend, when God gives you an assignment, it takes time. You won't get the whole picture all at once. It is a process. God will take you through your steps, phases, and challenges. Joseph did not go immediately from Potiphar's house to Pharaoh's palace. He had obstacles along the way. Satan will try to hinder you in any way that he can, but he is no match for our God! You may feel like throwing up your hands, but don't you dare give up! God will help you.

I am not saying that you will undergo the severity of hardships as Joseph did, but whatever your challenges, just remember, God will see you through them all. He will let you know when it is time to move forward. Don't go ahead of Him, and don't lag behind Him. You must flow with Him. His watchful eye will guide you every step of the way. Don't become discouraged or frustrated if at first your steps seem small and insignificant—just keep moving forward. Satan's attacks will come, as they did with Joseph, as they did with me, but God is greater. God was with Joseph, and better yet, He is in us: "...greater is he that is in you, than he that is in the world," (1 John 4:4). Joseph's story should be an inspiration to all of us. Yes, he suffered, but God's favor on his life far exceeded his hurts. God wants to help you! Won't you let Him? We were never created to be self-sufficient but rather to be God-dependent. We cannot handle life on our own. God is such a loving God, and He wants the best for us. Live your life to the fullest and keep God first. He will take you places that you never could have imagined. "For I know the thoughts that I think toward you, saith the LORD, thoughts of peace, and not of evil, to give you an expected end," (Jeremiah 29:11).

Be encouraged, God is long-suffering and He is not finished with you. Please continue to journey with me as we take a look at some of the Apostle Peter's ouches, hurts, and victories.

Chapter Two

Peter's Transformation

This section of this book is not intended to give an in-depth study into Peter's life, but rather hopes to underscore some of his ouches, hurts, and victories as he yielded himself to the work of the Lord. Peter, of course, was not the Lord's only disciple, but for the purpose of this story, our focus is on Peter.

The Apostle Peter could be described as one with an impulsive nature. Oftentimes he would react to situations before thinking things over. I guess you could say that Peter spoke his mind—right or wrong, he put it out there. It was obvious that he had character flaws. He was a man whom you could say reacted to his emotions much of the time. It's easy to be loud or aggressive or quiet or lazy when we allow our emotions to dictate to us. Peter's transformation was miraculous, to say the least. Jesus worked in him and through him, and he became a mighty man of God who wrote 1 Peter and 2 Peter in the New Testament of the Holy Bible—wow! My sisters, and brothers— there is hope for us!

Peter's character flaws did not prevent Jesus from using him. Even when we mess up, the Lord does not quit on us. "If ye be willing and obedient, ye shall eat the good of the land," (Isaiah 1:19). It does not say if we are willing, obedient, and perfect we shall eat the good of the land. It gives me great pleasure to know that God is a patient God who never gives up on us. Philippians 1:6 bears repeating, "Being confident of this very thing, that he which hath begun a good work in you will perform it until the day of Jesus Christ."

Before God ever called us, He already knew us. He knew us before we were formed in our mother's wombs (Jeremiah 1:5). Jesus knew Peter had some rough edges, and He knew that with Peter's cooperation, there would be nothing that Peter would not be able to accomplish in Him and through Him. The Lord knows how to smooth out our rough edges.

Some may have a tendency to criticize Peter, but I believe we, too, at times exhibit "Peter's mentality." How many times have we spoken out of turn, or acted inappropriately, said something that we later regretted, and had to pull our foot out of our mouths metaphorically speaking? How many times have we acted in haste, driven by our emotions when we should have waited, and the outcome would have been much more favorable?

Let's take a brief look at the life of Peter:

"And Jesus, walking by the sea of Galilee, saw two brethren, Simon called Peter, and Andrew his brother, casting a net into the sea: for they were fishers. And he saith unto them, Follow me, and I will make you fishers of men. And they straightway left their nets, and followed him."

Matthew 4:18-20

A Call to Serve

When Jesus called Peter, he was a fisherman whom I envisioned had a prosperous fishing business, along with his partners (see Luke 5:7,10). Given Peter's outspoken nature (Mark 8:32-33), I imagine it was Peter who took charge when disputes arose at sea.

So Peter walked away from his fishing business to follow Jesus. This was no small thing. He walked away from what I believe was a flourishing business. He not only walked away from a flourishing business but also from a position of power. I'm sure it was hard on Peter's flesh to walk away from the familiar lifestyle that he had known all of his life. Peter was well-secured in what he knew, and now he was about to embark upon the unknown. In faith, Peter joined up with Jesus to answer his call.

Peter had a strong and sometimes abrasive personality, but it did not stop Jesus from using him. In fact, he became one of Jesus' right-hand disciples. Many people would be tempted to draw back from such a strong personality trait—but not Jesus. Beloved, Jesus sees so much more in us, than we see in ourselves. It is not our occupation that determines how the Lord will use us—it is not our degrees, or our flawed character. He is not impressed by our credentials, nor is he disappointed by our failures—" ...for the LORD seeth not as man seeth; for man looketh on the outward appearance, but the LORD looketh on the heart," (1 Samuel 16:7). He sees beyond our self-imposed limitations to what we could become. Oftentimes, what we call success is not success at all, and what we call failure, is not failure at all. A successful life is not just about our personal accomplishments, but rather about our selfless contributions to the Kingdom of God. It is about how we can bless someone else. Having the Lord Jesus with us is what really makes us successful!

As Peter began to follow Jesus, I believe Peter was captivated as Jesus taught the multitudes the Word of God, (Matthew 4:23). Peter witnessed Jesus perform many miracles. Jesus healed the sick, (Matthew 12:15); fed the hungry, (Matthew 14:19-21); opened blinded eyes, (Mark 10:51-52); opened deaf ears, (Mark 7:32-35); raised the dead, (Luke 7:12-15) and cast out demons, (Matthew 8:31-32)—to name some of the miracles that He performed. "And there are also many other things which Jesus did, the which, if they should be written every one, I suppose that even the world itself could not contain the books that should be written. Amen," (John 21:25).

One of the personal miracles that Peter witnessed was when Jesus healed Peter's mother-in-law. "And when Jesus was come into Peter's house, he saw his wife's mother laid, and sick of a fever. And he touched her hand, and the fever left her: and she arose, and ministered unto them,"(Matthew 8:14-15).

I believe as Peter witnessed Jesus performing miracles day in and day out, Peter's faith began to rise to the point where he believed that he could walk on water—just like Jesus.

Have Faith in God

Jesus was walking on the water near the apostles' boat during the early morning hours, and they were afraid for they thought He was a ghost. Jesus told them not to be afraid, as He called out to them.

And Peter answered him and said, Lord, if it be thou, bid me come unto thee on the water. And he said, Come. And when Peter was come down out of the ship, he walked on the water, to go to Jesus. But when he saw the wind boisterous, he was afraid; and beginning to sink, he cried, saying, Lord, save me. And immediately Jesus stretched forth his hand, and caught him, and said unto him. O thou of little faith, wherefore didst thou doubt?

Matthew 14:28-31

Here was Peter doing something that no other human had done, but he did not fully accomplish his task because he took his eyes off of Jesus. When he looked at his surroundings and saw the effect of the boisterous winds, he began to sink. Of course, no one can take away the fact that Peter walked on the water. He was not the only disciple in the boat, but he was the only one bold enough to get out of the boat. That says a lot about Peter's determined attitude. He seized the opportunity to emulate Jesus, but soon became distracted by his surroundings. Peter had enough faith to get out of the boat, which was evident by his action, but he allowed doubt and fear to get in the way. Jesus told him that he had little faith. He did not say that he did not have any faith. I encourage you to read the encounter in Matthew 17: 19-20, as Jesus talked to his disciples about faith and unbelief. Peter's faith got him out of the boat, but doubt hindered him from staying on top of the water.

My friend, as long as we keep our focus on Jesus, we can tread the troubled waters of life. The moment we take our eyes off of Him we find ourselves in trouble. Jesus reached out to Peter and saved him from drowning. Jesus is still reaching out to save the lost. He, however, gives us free will to choose whom we will serve.

Let's take a look at another one of Peter's encounters when he began to rebuke Jesus:

"And he began to teach them, that the Son of man must suffer many things, and be rejected of the elders, and of the chief priests, and scribes, and be killed, and after three days rise again. And he spake that saying openly. And Peter took him, and began to rebuke him. But when he had turned about and looked on his disciples, he rebuked Peter, saying, Get thee behind me, Satan: for thou savourest not the things that be of God, but the things that be of men."

Mark 8:31-33

Peter apparently thought that he would rescue Jesus from His eventual death. It must have been quite a shock to Peter's ego when Jesus said, "Get thee behind me, Satan." Can you imagine—Peter thinking that he was somehow protecting Jesus from what Jesus was destined to suffer on the cross! Jesus was not directly calling Peter "Satan," but He knew that Satan had influenced Peter's words. Jesus knew His mission on this earth, and not Peter, not the devil or anyone could stop Him from fulfilling His mission.

Peter, no doubt had a nostalgic moment of how he would step in to protect his crew from attackers at sea, and lost sight that this was Jesus, not his crew. Jesus did not need Peter's help. It was Peter who needed Jesus' help. Jesus would be the Great Protector, not Peter!

It was this same Peter who earlier told Jesus that he would be willing to die for Him when others would be ashamed of Him (Mark 14:66-72). Later Peter denied having ever known Jesus when he thought his life would be in jeopardy.

It was this same Peter who drew his sword and cut off the high priest's servant's right ear when they came to arrest Jesus in the garden leading up to His crucifixion (John 18:10). As you can see, Peter experienced many "Ouch! It hurts" circumstances. Jesus was patient with Peter, and He is patient with us! Jesus never gave up on Peter. He helped him through all of his challenges. He is willing to help you.

Peter had to learn to trust Jesus, and not to be dependent upon himself. Christians sometimes give themselves too much credit. God has empowered Born-Again Believers with super natural abilities, and by no means are we weaklings—but we are who we are because of who Jesus is in us! We must never lose focus that it is the Lord who propels us. It is only through His grace and mercy that causes us to triumph to victory. Without Him we are nothing! All of the glory, honor, and praise belongs to Him. "But we all, with open face beholding as in a glass the glory of the Lord, are changed into the same image from glory to glory, even as by the Spirit of the Lord. 2 Corinthians 3:18"

Let's fast forward to the later years of Peter's ministry and see his transformation.

Inside Transformation, Outside Manifestation

Peter's life was transformed after he received the promised Holy Spirit. He became a spiritual giant, who was bold and courageous in the right way. He began to see Jesus with his heart and not just with head knowledge. Peter did powerful works in the Kingdom of God, but not without cost. My sisters and brothers, I do not wish you to be misinformed. Even while walking with the Lord, you will face challenges, and some will seem almost unbearable, but don't faint in doing good, Jesus will help you. "And let us not be weary in well doing: for in due season we shall reap, if we faint not," (Galatians 6:9). You may have to recharge, but don't give up. In the natural, it would be impossible to live the Christian life—but, thank God for the precious Holy Spirit, our Helper Who resides on the inside of born-again believers!

Peter preached to the masses, letting them know that Jesus had been crucified but God raised Jesus from the dead, and He is now seated on the right hand of the Father interceding for us. Peter's message so convicted the people that some three thousand gave their lives to the Lord (Acts 2:41). Peter was so anointed, that the sick were laid on cots in the streets and Peter, through Jesus healed them. (Acts 5:15.

When he would not stop preaching the gospel and healing the sick, he was beaten and thrown into prison. Emotionally, this can be devastating, but the good news is that Peter was not doing this in his own strength; he had supernatural help from the Lord. When Peter and the other disciples went through tribulations, in Acts 5:41, we find these words, "And they departed from the presence of the council, rejoicing that they were counted worthy to suffer shame for His name."

Here is something else to encourage you—when Peter started out with Jesus, he made many mistakes. As he began to put his trust in the Lord, he grew strong in faith and his life began to change. If Jesus could use Peter, surely, He can use us. Much of the time, He uses those whom others would not be willing to take a second look. Society would label them as hopeless, and the least likely to succeed, but The Lord sees great potential!

"For ye see your calling, brethren, how that not many wise men after the flesh, not many mighty, not many noble, are called: But God hath chosen the foolish things of the world to confound the wise; and God hath chosen the weak things of the world to confound the things which are mighty; And base things of the world, and things which are despised, hath God chosen, yea, and things which are not, to bring to nought things that are: That no flesh should glory in his presence. "

1 Corinthians 1:26-29

Proclaim the Good News!

God is still looking for followers with willing hearts to proclaim the Gospel, the Good News—that He indeed is a good God! Many believe that God is mad at them for their disobedience. The Scripture clearly tells us in Romans 2:4 that it is the goodness of God that lead men to repentance, and John 10:10 lets us know that it is Satan who comes to steal, to kill, and to destroy. Disobedience will, however, open the door for Satan to come in, and he will destroy you if he can. Jesus came that we might have life and have it more abundantly. Thank God for His grace and His mercy.

As others have said, and I agree, God's grace, does not give us a license to sin. On the contrary, we are to live holy lives because God is holy. When we become born-again Jesus exchanges our sinful nature and gives us His holiness (He brews 10:10). He takes our unrighteousness and makes us righteous (1 Corinthians 1:30 and 2 Corinthians 5:21).

Living under grace does not mean that we are to live any kind of way, rather it is because of the Lord's grace that we are able to live holy lives. God's grace is His unmerited favor that He has given to us. It is not earned, nor do we deserve it. It is a gift from God! Hallelujah to His holy name! The Lord will let us know when we begin to veer off course. He knows how to correct us and when to correct us. "My son, despise not the chastening of the LORD; neither be weary of his corrections: For whom the LORD loveth he correcteth; even as a father the son in whom he delighted," (Proverbs 3:11-12). "Now no chastening for the present seemeth to be joyous, but grievous: nevertheless afterward it yielded the peaceable fruit of righteousness unto them which are exercised thereby," (Hebrews 12:11).

Peter, in his weakness, still had the stamina to step out of the boat. For today's believers, "stepping out of the boat" would be to proclaim the Good News—the Gospel of Jesus Christ to the world. Not many are willing to bear the criticism that comes with doing so. It is not popular to talk about the grace of God without being persecuted. "Yea, and all that will live godly in Christ Jesus shall suffer persecution," (2 Timothy 3:12). Peter failed to accomplish his mission successfully of walking on the water; however, his efforts cannot be discounted. He had done what others were afraid to do. He was not the only disciple in the boat, but he was the only one who got out of the boat. When you choose to stay in your boat, you limit your opportunity to make a difference in this world.

It's Time to Get Out of Your Boat

My sisters and brothers, do not let anyone, Satan, or even your own negative thoughts and words, rob you of a life worth living. You will never realize your full potential until you are willing to get out of your boat, your comfort zone, your state of complacency, and go for your dream! What if you succeed?

Who wants to live a life of mediocrity when you can do so much better? There is no real satisfaction in mediocrity, and there are certainly no limitations in God. Peter's journey was an extraordinary one. However, it did not happen overnight, nor did it happen by accident. Peter had to cooperate with the Lord. He made mistakes, but Jesus was with Peter, and

He helped him through them all. He wants to use you to your maximum potential. Are you willing to be used mightily by The Lord? If your answer is yes, then you must be willing to get out of your boat and not to allow your past disappointments, hurts, and failures stop you from fulfilling your God-given call! Someone is depending on you, and you might be the only one that can lead him or her to Christ. What a privilege and an honor it is to be used by the Lord.

It is my prayer that you have been encouraged by Peter's story—come, let us continue our journey with Jesus' dear friends, Mary, Martha, and Lazarus as they experienced hurt, disappointment and victory.

Chapter Three

The Story of Mary, Martha, and Lazarus

We do not live in a perfect world, and you can be assured that difficult times will come. It profits us nothing, however, to take on the role of a complainer or to blame others for our misfortunes.

"Then said Martha unto Jesus, Lord, if thou hadst been here, my brother had not died,"

John 11:21

Often it is through life adversities that we realize that we need help from others and most assuredly from God. When our bodies began to break down and discomfort sets in, we look for relief. Some may take over-the-counter pills. Some may seek immediate medical attention. Others may pray their way through. In other words, we do whatever is necessary to rid our bodies of sickness and disease. We know that sickness is never a good thing and if left untreated, it could lead to an early death. It is not God's will for His children to experience these "life-stealers." Why do I refer to sickness, disease, and death as life-stealers you may ask? Let's take a look at 3 John verse 2, "Beloved, I wish above all things that thou mayest prosper and be in health, even as thou soul prospereth." In 1 Corinthians 15:26, "The last enemy that shall be destroyed is death." Of course, we know that eventually, we must depart this life because of Adam's and Eve's disobedience in the garden of Eden. Life is precious and while we are still on this earth, our earnest desire should be to honor God with our daily living.

Put Your Trust in Jesus

Like Martha and Mary, we do not understand everything that happens in our lives. We won't experience a perfect life until we get to Heaven. The result of Adam's and Eve's sin causes us to live in a fallen world. We must understand that bad things do happen, even to Christians. Satan hates God and he hates us and would like nothing more than to destroy us and to sift us as wheat. "And the Lord said, Simon, Simon, behold, Satan hath desired to have you, that he may sift you as wheat: But I have prayed for thee, that thy faith fail not...," (Luke 22:31-32). No matter the hurt and the pain we may encounter along life' s journey, we must keep our trust in Jesus and remain steadfast in faith. Even when we do not understand the whys of everything, we must never lose faith in our Heavenly Father who loves us unconditionally and promise that He would never leave us or forsake us. The storms of life will come, but we can get through them with the help of the Lord. His love will see us through anything. I love this Scripture, "Fear thou not; for I am with thee: be not dismayed; for I am thy God: I will strengthen thee; yea, I will help thee; yea, I will uphold thee with the right hand of my righteousness," (Isaiah 41: 10). What a powerful and comforting promise!

When Jesus heard the news that Lazarus was sick, He continued His journey, for He knew the plan that His Heavenly Father had for Lazarus, and it would result in victory. Jesus was not disturbed by negative reports. His eyes were fixed on His Heavenly Father and He refused to be distracted. In fact, Jesus stayed another two days where He was when He received the message of Lazarus' illness. I encourage you to read John 11 in its entirety for a better understanding of this story.

When Martha found out that Jesus was finally on His way, she ran to meet Him and immediately let Jesus know how disappointed and hurt she was that He had not come in time, and Lazarus was now dead. Jesus had compassion on Martha, and assured her that Lazarus would rise again; He let her know that He meant now, and not at the resurrection at the last day as she had thought. Jesus said to her, "I Am the Resurrection!" He only asked that Martha would believe and have faith in Him. She told Him that she knew God would do whatever He asked of Him.

The sisters loved Jesus as did Lazarus, but when Lazarus died, they blamed Jesus because He did not show up when they expected Him. Isn't this how many people react today? They pray and say that they trust God, but when things don't work out the way that they thought they should, they blame God. Beloved, some things just happen, and some things happen at the hands of the enemy, or from our own bad decisions, but God always wants the best for us.

When tragedy strikes, many Christians believe the Lord had a hand in it. They don't seem to remember Scripture like Psalms 91 that promises us His protection. Why then do we experience bad things in life? 1 Corinthian 13, lets us know that we see darkly through the glass right now. We do not have answers for everything that happens, but I do know that God has a good plan for each of us, and I believe we, too, have a hand in the outcome of our lives. God gives us choices. "I call heaven and earth to record this day against you, that 1 have set before you life and death, blessing and cursing: therefore choose life, that both thou and thy seed may live," (Deuteronomy 30:19). "Death and life are in the power of the tongue: and they that love it shall eat the fruit thereof," (Proverbs 18:21). Proverbs 6:2 states, "Thou art snared with the words of thy mouth, thou art taken with the words of thy mouth."

"For verily I say unto you, That whosoever shall say unto this mountain, Be thou removed, and be thou cast into the sea; and shall not doubt in his heart, but shall believe that those things which he saith shall come to pass; he shall have

whatsoever he saith. Therefore I say unto you, What things soever ye desire, when ye pray, believe that ye receive them, and ye shall have them. "

Mark 11:23-24

Do you trust the Lord Jesus with your life? Is your life one of surrender to Him? How many times have you blamed Him for your mishaps? Do you still trust Him when life makes no sense? Jesus wants to be involved in every aspect of your life. Go to Him for help. You may have to do it with tears running down your face, but go to Him. He does not want you to try to run your own life. The weight of it is too heavy and it will crush you! Don't stay in your hurt—it will destroy you. Have faith in God. The Scripture says in Isaiah 26:3, "Thou wilt keep him in perfect peace, whose mind is stayed on thee: because he trusteth in thee."

The Promise Fulfilled

When Jesus saw Martha and Mary and the crowd that had gathered, He had compassion on them and asked to see where Lazarus was buried. He knew that God would raise Lazarus from the dead, but He prayed to His Father for the sake of the people, so that they would see the power of God manifest. As soon as Jesus gave instruction to roll the stone away from Lazarus' tomb, Martha suddenly yelled out that Lazarus had been dead for four days and his odor would be offensive. How quickly had she reverted back to her old way of thinking, and soon forgot the promise of Jesus that Lazarus would be raised from the grave.

This is the way many Christians respond today. The Lord has given us His precious promises found in the Holy Bible— His love letter to us, but still some doubt because they cannot always see how things will turn out. This is when trust comes in; believe by faith!

Martha did not have to tell Jesus about the attributes of a decayed body. He already knew everything about it. He knew that nothing was impossible with God. The odor was not important to Him. We all give off offensive odors to the Lord when we disobey Him, but His precious blood takes them away! "I, even I, am he that blotteth out thy transgressions for mine own sake, and will not remember thy sins," (Isaiah 43: 25). Lazarus would come forth untainted. The power of God would cleanse him. When Jesus called Lazarus, he came forward in his grave clothes with the death napkin still on his face. Jesus instructed the people to "loose him" and to let him go.

We have a better covenant with God than did Martha, Mary, and Lazarus. Jesus had not yet gone to the cross, died, and been resurrected. We have been loosed from the sting of death. "Oh death, where is thy sting? O grave, where is thy victory?" (1 Corinthians 15: 55). We can boldly proclaim the goodness of the Lord and shine as beacons of light in dark places. We don't have to stay in our hurts any longer. Jesus has paved the way for us to live abundant lives! Hallelujah to His holy name! When Jesus went to the cross, He said, "Father, it is finished!" He paid the ultimate price for all of our hurts. He has made a way of escape through His own precious blood that was shed at Calvary for the remission of our sins. Jesus has done it all! For the non- Christian who may be reading this book, my prayer is that you will believe and receive the finished work of Jesus at the cross. Jesus called out to Lazarus and he came forward. Jesus is calling out to you; will you come forward? Will you walk in the path of righteousness that He has prepared for you, and will you point others to Christ? There is a Prayer Guide at the end of this book, should you need it. Don't despair when times are tough. The Lord promised to take care of his children no matter what we may go through. "Nay, in all these things we are more than conquerors through him that loved us," The Lord honors his covenant (Romans 8:37).

God's Amazing Love

"No evil shall compass you, nor shall any plagues come near you that I won't step in and deliver you from, says the Lord of Host. My Word is Who I Am. My Word will stand forever. Come my child and follow Me. Let Me show you that which you long to see come to pass in your life. I can do it if you would obey My Word, and follow me. Let me show you what life is, to really live a life that would bring joy to Him who created you. No one else can show you, and lead you down the path of joy in the Lord. My eyes roam to and fro over my earth to show myself strong in the man, woman, boy or girl who would commit themselves unto Me."

These words were coming to me so rapidly as I was writing on this portion of the book that I could hardly keep up with typing them. I believe they were divinely inspired.

What do you do when you find yourself in a barren place? Hannah found herself in such a place. Let's take a look at her story and see how God worked in her life.

Chapter Four

Hannah's Story

This is an awesome story of the love of God, and how He answered the prayer of a woman in despair. Please keep in mind that this is an Old Testament story. Hannah did not have the covenant that New Testament believers have.

"Now there was a certain man of Ramathaim-zophim, of mount Epharaim, and his name was Elkanah, the son of Jeroham, the son of Elihu, the son of Tohu, the son of Zuph, an Ephrathite: And he had two wives; the name of the one was Hannah, and the name of the other Peninnah: and Peninnah had children, but Hannah had no children."

1 Samuel 1:1-2

Beloved, life can be quite challenging at times. It can come at you hard, and if you are not grounded in the Word of God, it can knock you off of your feet! Even with being grounded, it can certainly shake you to your very core. There are times when things seem to be going just fine and the next thing you know, "Wham!" you are hit with a situation and you know there is no way that you could possibly come out of it without God's intervention. You, who were once so vibrant and full of life and felt as if you were on top of the world, now feel as if the world is on top of you and "Ouch!" does it hurt. Your emotions are all over the place. Some days seem better than others, but still you don't have the joy you once had. What happened, you asked yourself? You must remember that feelings are forever changing depending on what is going on in your life. You cannot rely on them. You must rely on the

Word of God or else the enemy will come in like a flood and sabotage your life. Hannah did not have the precious Holy Spirit living on the inside of her as new covenant believers have. The enemy worked through Peninnah in an attempt to destroy Hannah's self-worth and to strip her of her dignity. Peninnah gloated over the fact that God had not yet given Hannah children.

Hannah, no doubt from time to time would look around at the nice amenities in her home, but those things, as magnificent as they were, could not fill the emptiness that she felt on the inside. No materialistic thing or amount of money could give her a child. As time went on Hannah, no doubt, began to compare her life to that of her neighbors. They didn't seem to have any struggles. You admire this kind of family and you wonder what happened to yours. You don't mean to compare your life to others, but you find yourself doing so anyway. This is not a wise thing to do according to 2 Corinthians 10:12. Now your hurt intensifies, and you look back over your life, and your greatest desire to have a family seems impossible and you remain barren. What do you do?

Cast Your Cares on the Lord

You know the enemy must have spoken to Hannah's mind over and over with lies that she would never have a child. Here she was married to a man who loved her very much, but still she was unable to have a child. She felt ashamed and embarrassed. The Scripture says that each year Elkanah would take his family up to Shiloh for their sacrificial offering and worship to the Lord. Peninnah would provoke Hannah to tears. I believe Hannah lived in constant torment of Peninnah's negative comments and behavior. Her words would hurt so badly that Hannah would just cry. Her husband could not understand what Hannah was going through. He believed that she should have been happy, even if they could not have children together. "Then said Elkanah her husband to her, Hannah, why weepest thou? and why eatest thou not? and why is thy heart grieved? am not I better to thee than ten sons?" (1 Samuel 1:8). Hannah longed for a child and she was not willing to let go of her dream.

Have you ever been there? In that barren place, I mean. You know there is more to life than what you are living. You say to yourself, "something is missing" and "I don't feel fulfilled." You try to fill your schedule with all kinds of activities. Temporarily, you may have some satisfaction, but as time passes you find that there is no real joy or passion in what you are doing. You find yourself just going through the motions. What do you do now? You feel as if life is passing you by, and your opportunity to find your true passion grows dimmer with each passing day. Before you can come to grips with one month, another has sneaked in. You take another look, and the year is almost gone. You ask the question, "Lord, what happened?" "My vision, my dream, my passion, still has not come to pass!" You begin to wonder if it will ever manifest or is it too late. Now you feel stuck in a barren place, a place of hurt, a place of disappointment–an unproductive state. What do you do? How do you turn things around with the remaining time that you have left on the earth? The hurt, the disappointment, and the sheer pain of it seems almost unbearable at times.

I have good news for you! God is able to turn your dismal situation around. Cast your cares on the Lord. He is able to restore your joy and to bring you out with the victory. The scripture says in James 4:2, "... ye have not, because ye ask not." Hannah made up her mind that she was going to seek the Lord with her whole heart. She no longer had time to procrastinate. Her future was on the line! She knew what was in her heart and she refused to give in to defeat. Romans 8:31 states, "...If God be for us, who can be against us?" Again, let me remind you that we have a much better covenant with the Lord than Hannah had. We have God the Father, God the Son, and God the Holy Spirit living on the inside of us!

Stand Your Ground

When Hannah got fed up with the lies of her adversary, she made up her mind that the very next trip to Shiloh, she would get before the Lord and pour out her heart to Him. She was tired of not being able to eat or to sleep. She was tired of being laughed at and taunted by Peninnah. She was tired of the seemingly endless tears. Hannah knew that if God did not help her, she would never have a child. She had to step out by faith to find out by faith that her God was indeed a prayer answering God and true to His word. Her heart was heavy, but she had a made-up mind that nothing would stop her from seeking the Lord in her desperate time of need. She knew she had to persevere through her hurt and to stand her ground believing God would grant her petition, because He is a good God. Hannah refused to be intimated any longer. What about you?

Misunderstood, But Determined

When you get a determined mind to seek after the Lord, you will be misunderstood and criticized. Your feelings will get hurt. You may feel like a lone ranger, but don't give up! Keep on trusting God no matter the criticism, no matter the ouches, no matter the hurts; keep at it. He will bring you out with the victory.

Eli, the high priest had mistaken Hannah's behavior as a state of intoxication. Hannah knew the burden that she was carrying was beyond her ability to solve. Hannah took a gigantic leap of faith, and promised God, that if He would give her a male child, she would give him back to be used by God for the rest of his life. What a promise; what faith! After Hannah had prayed, she felt as if her burden had been lifted, and she was on top of the world, instead of being crushed by it. After Hannah explained herself to Eli, he blessed her and told her to go in peace and may God grant her petition.

1 Samuel 9:18

"And they rose up in the morning early, and worshipped before the LORD, and returned, and came to their house in Ramah: and Elkanah knew Hannah his wife; and the LORD remembered her. Wherefore it came to pass, when the time was come about after Hannah had conceived, that she bare a son, and called his name Samuel, saying, Because I have asked him of the LORD."

1 Samuel 1:19-20

Hannah kept her promise to God. She did not go back for the yearly sacrifice and worship at Shiloh until she had weaned her son. When Samuel was weaned, Hannah took him to the temple to Eli. God honored Hannah's commitment and blessed her with several more children! Hannah rejoiced in the Lord for His goodness and kindness. Hannah knew it was God's strength that brought her through her barrenness. She saw God move mightily in her life. Now Hannah's song of praise to God was one of thanksgiving. She saw her God as her rock and one of knowledge, and there is no God like Him. Those who thought they could hold her down were now brought down by Him. She, who was down and weak in strength, saw God lift her up out of her despair. Hannah, who once was ashamed and embarrassed, now held her head up high because God had vindicated her. He had delivered her from her state of barrenness. Her song of high praise was: "He raiseth up the poor out of the dust, and lifteth up the beggar from the dunghill, to set them among princes, and to make them inherit the throne of glory: for the pillars of the earth are the LORD'S, and he hath set the world upon them. He will keep the feet of his saints, and the wicked shall be silent in darkness; for by strength shall no man prevail. The adversaries of the LORD shall be broken to pieces, out of heaven shall he thunder upon them: the LORD shall judge the ends of the earth; and he shall give strength unto his king, and exalt the horn of His anointed."

1 Samuel 2:8-10

Stay the Course

The enemy will fight you with everything that he has to keep your dream, your vision, your greatest desire from coming to pass. He knows that if he can defeat you in your mind, he can stop you from fulfilling your calling. He will use whatever deceptions he can. Lies and fear are two of his main tactics. We only have a short time in the earth to fulfill our assignment. "But, beloved, be not ignorant of this one thing, that one day is with the Lord as a thousand years, and a thousand years as one day," (2 Peter 3:8). Hannah would bring forth greatness. Her son, Samuel would be God's prophet—His spokesman, if you will. What you have on the inside of you can have tremendous influence in this world. God wants to use you in a mighty way. Again, I ask, what is that Godly dream—that vision—that deep desire in your heart? Let God deliver you from your state of barrenness and bring you to your place of victory. Let Him birth greatness through you and multiply in your life. You may see yourself in a barren place right now, but the good news is that you don't have to stay there. God loves you!

Have faith in God. Abram is a great example of how God can work on your behalf. God won't fail you. Abram, later called Abraham, left a lifestyle that he was well acquainted with to obey God to sojourn to a foreign land as God led him every step of the way. Let's take a look at some of his ouches, hurts, and victories—this man of great faith!

Chapter Five

Abraham: The Man of Great Faith

I encourage you to read the account of Abraham. This story epitomizes God's faithfulness to His children and shows how good God is, even when we fall short of fully obeying Him. Abram was instructed by God to leave the familiar to go to the unfamiliar. He was an ordinary man who put his faith in God. When God spoke to Abram to leave his father's house, and even his own country to journey to a place that He would show him as he journeyed, took an enormous amount of faith (Genesis 12:1). Like you and me, Abraham had some "Ouch! It hurts" moments in his life, but God's grace and mercy sustained him, and brought him out with the victory. We will take a look at some of his challenges and victories in the impending paragraphs.

You Are Not Too Old for God's Army

Abram was seventy-five years old when God spoke to him to leave his father's house and his relatives to go to a place that He would show him. At Abram's age, many believe they have lived their best years and have nothing more to contribute. In essence, they seem to say, "I'm seventy-five and my life is over." What a wrong mindset! Caleb at the age of eighty-five had great strength—even to do battle when necessary (Joshua 14:11). Moses was one hundred and twenty years old when he died; his eyesight was not dim, nor his natural force abated (Deuteronomy 34:7). Psalm 92 tells us that the righteous shall flourish and bring forth fruit in old age. God has graciously endowed each of us with talents to be used to build His Kingdom. Of course, with each passing day we are closer to leaving this earth to take our rightful place with Jesus, our Savior. Should we live to be one hundred and twenty, it would be but a drop in the bucket compared to eternity!

Why not believe God for long life since Jesus has redeemed us from the curse, according to Galatians 3:13. Death is an enemy (1 Corinthians 15:26). Why not make the most out of your life, and leave a legacy that would honor God. Remember, with God, all things are possible to him that believe (Mark 9:23).

Obedience is Key to Your Victory

Like Abram, we must be willing to follow God's plan. Abram did not know where he was going. God did not reveal the whole picture to him all at once. In fact, He did not reveal anything to Abram. He just told him to go and He would show him as he went. Usually, we want to know all of the details before we move forward. That is not faith. We must trust God. A right heart and obedience is key to walking in God's promises. Our faith walk will take us one step at a time.

To reiterate a previous point, man looks at the outward appearance, but God looks at the heart. Man often ignores those in whom God sees great potential. Man says you are too old, and God says, you are just right. Man says you aren't smart enough, and God says you are just right for the job. Man says you don't look the part, and God says your heart is right towards Him. Who will you believe? God is saying follow Me, and I will transform your life. Who would not want this? Many get caught up in their own agendas, failing to seek God's agenda for their lives. They find themselves going through needless hurts and disappointments. It hurts when life beats us down. Have you ever asked God what His plan is for your life? Please do not become so busy with trying to live your life that you fail to find out from God what

He wants you to do. Why not anchor yourself in Scripture like Psalm 25:1-5:

"Unto thee, O LORD, do I lift up my soul. O my God, I trust in thee: let me not be ashamed, let not mine enemies triumph over me. Yea, let none that wait on thee be ashamed: let them be ashamed which transgress without cause. Shew me thy ways, O LORD; teach my thy paths. Lead me in thy truth and teach me: for thou art the God of my salvation; on thee do I wait all the day."

Let's take a look at God's promises to Abram:

"And I will make of thee a great nation, and I will bless thee, and make thy name great; and thou shalt be a blessing: And I will bless them that bless thee, and curse him that curseth thee: and in thee shall all families of the earth be blessed."

Genesis 12:2-3

God wants His children blessed so they can be a blessing to others and God gets all the glory, all the honor and all the praise for it.

Flawed, But Willing

We know from scripture that Abram made mistakes, but he had a heart for God. "And he believed in the LORD; and he counted it to him for righteousness," (Genesis 15:6). God's instructions to Abram in Genesis 12 was to leave his father's house and his relatives to go to a place that He would show him. Abram took Lot, his nephew, with him. As he continued his journey, he added others, but God did not reprove Abram or tell him to send anyone back. Instead He prospered him along the way.

Abram's character flaws did not stop God from using him. During his journey, Abram lied to the Egyptians that Sarai was his sister for fear of losing his own life. True, Sarai was his half sister, but she was also his wife. According to the Levitical Law (Leviticus 18:9), Abram should not have married his half sister in the first place. God wants His children blessed so they can be a blessing to others and God gets all the glory, all the honor and all the praise for it.

There was a famine in the land, and Abram and Sarai had come to Egypt to purchase food. Sarai was a beautiful woman.

"Therefore it shall come to pass, when the Egyptians shall see thee, that they shall say, This is his wife: and they will kill me, but they will save thee alive. Say, I pray thee, thou art my sister: that it may be well with me for thy sake; and my soul shall live because of thee. And it came to pass, that, when Abram was come into Egypt, the Egyptians beheld the woman that she was very fair. The princes also of Pharaoh saw her, and commended her before Pharaoh: and the woman was taken into Pharaoh's house."

Genesis 12:12-15

God intervened with a mighty hand and delivered Sarai out of the Egyptians' hands before any harm had come to her. The Egyptians rebuked Abram for lying, and gave Sarai back, and sent them on their way with an abundance of goods (Genesis 12- 13). In Genesis 20, Abram did the same thing to Abimelech, King of Gerar. He withheld the fact that Sarai was his wife. He led them to believe that she was only his sister to spare his life, as he had done with the Egyptians. God dealt with Abimelech in a dream to let him know that the woman he had taken into his harem was married to His prophet, Abram. Abimelech feared God and immediately had Sarai removed from his harem. Abimelech never came near Sarai because again, God intervened. Abimelech rebuked Abram for what happened, and sent him and Sarai away with an abundance of goods. He also gave Abram a thousand pieces of silver to compensate Sarai and to vindicate her honor.

You would have thought that God would have really come down hard on Abram for his deceitfulness—instead, God continued to guide Abram with His grace and mercy. God was not yet imputing sin against them. "Blessed is the man to whom the Lord will not impute sin for we say that faith was reckoned to Abraham for righteousness," (Romans 4:8-9).

Abram and Sarai Lacked One Thing

The favor of God on Abram's life had caused him to prosper plentifully, but there was one thing that Abram and Sarai lacked, they had no children. It was an "Ouch! It hurts" circumstance that was beyond their ability to change, and they were now old in years.

"After these things the word of the LORD came unto Abram in a vision, saying, Fear not, Abram: I am thy shield, and thy exceeding great reward. And Abram said, Lord GOD, what wilt thou give me, seeing I go childless, and the steward of my house is this Eliezer of Damascus? And Abram said, Behold, to me thou hast given no seed: and, lo, one born in my house is mine heir. And, behold, the word of the LORD came unto him, saying, This shall not be thine heir; but he that shall come forth out of thine own bowels shall be thine heir."

Genesis 15:1-4

God changed Abram's name to Abraham (a father of many nations or multitudes) and Sarai to Sarah (princess). As the story continues, the promise did not manifest in Abraham's and Sarah's life until twenty-five years later. During the interim, Sarah became anxious and intervened in a negative way. She insisted that her husband sleep with her maid, Hagar (See Genesis 16:2-4). Hagar conceived and bore a male child, and his name was Ishmael, but he was not the promised child. Abraham and Sarah lacked patience and took matters into their own hands. This was not the Godly solution! Isn't this just like so many people? They become impatient during the wait and try to help God out—only to create a mess! Instead of resting in God's promises, they lean to their own understanding, which ultimately leads to disaster. My friend, God is true to His Word. "The Lord is not slack concerning his promise, as some men count slackness; but is longsuffering to usward. " (2 Peter 3:9). "God is not a man, that he should lie; neither the son of man, that he should repent: hath he said, and shall he not do it? or hath he spoken, and shall he not make it good?" (Numbers 23:19). You can rest assured if He has spoken it, it will come to pass. Why not do it God's way?

Hagar and Ishmael, It's Time to Leave

Sarah was ninety years old. (Genesis 17:17). Abraham was one hundred years old when the promised child, Isaac was born (Genesis 21:5). What a miracle! Their beloved child had finally arrived. Isaac would be the seed of Abraham. After Isaac was born, Sarah wanted Hagar and Ishmael out of her house.

"And the thing was very grievous in Abraham's sight because of his son. And God said unto Abraham, Let it not be grievous in thy sight because of the lad, and because of thy bond woman; in all that Sarah hath said unto thee, hearken unto her voice; for in Isaac shall thy seed be called. And also of the son of the bond woman will I make a nation, because he is thy seed. "

Genesis 21:11-13

Abraham loved Ishmael. He got up early in the morning and packed bread and a bottle of water and put it on Hagar's shoulder and she and Ishmael left Abraham's and Sarah's home. Hagar found herself in the wilderness of Beersheba (Genesis 21:14). When the boy's water had run out, Hagar withdrew from him because she did not want to watch him die. God's angel spoke from heaven to Hagar to let her know that God had heard Ishmael's cry. God told Hagar that He would make a great nation out of Ishmael. God never turned his back on Ishmael because he was the son of Abraham. God spared the life of Hagar and Ishmael and provided for them.

Even though Abraham and Sarah made mistakes, God worked through these flawed vessels to bring forth His promise. He never changed his mind towards them, and He won't change His mind towards you. Abraham and Sarah were not able to escape the consequences of their bad decision, but God remained faithful to them. He never reneges on his promises!

As we continue to trust God, our faith grows stronger and stronger. When God instructed Abraham to make the ultimate sacrifice, which was to lay Isaac on the alter to show forth his love for Him, Abraham passed the test (Genesis 22). God was pleased to see that Abraham loved Him more than he loved Isaac. God had the angel from heaven to speak to Abraham to stay his knife from coming down on Isaac and instructed him not to harm Isaac in any way. When Abraham looked around, there was a ram caught in the thicket, and he sacrificed the ram to God. Abraham's trust was in God and he was not moved by his circumstances. I believe Abraham was so focused on God that he refused to give in to fear, but instead operated in great faith. "By faith Abraham, when he was tried, offered up Isaac: and he that had received the promises offered up his only begotten son, of whom it was said, That in Isaac shall all thy seed be called: Accounting that God was able to raise him up, even from the dead; from whence also he received him in a figure," (Hebrews 11:17-19). Abraham had learned to put his trust in God wholeheartedly. Even if Isaac had died, Abraham believed that God would have raised him from the dead. God honored Abraham's faith. God provided a ram to take the place of Abraham's son. God knew that one day He would sacrifice His own Son to take our place. What love God has for us! Abraham and Isaac returned to the men who were waiting for them at the foot of the mountain— just as Abraham had said (Genesis 22:5). The Scripture says, Abraham believed God, and I encourage you to do the same.

Let us continue our journey. How do you move forward when life has given you a raw deal and the hurt is almost unbearable? Let us take a look at Naomi's and Ruth's circumstances.

Chapter Six

You Can Get Back Up Again!

After Naomi's husband and sons died, she returned to Bethlehem, but more importantly, she returned to her God. She desperately longed to be back in His presence.

"Now it came to pass in the days when the judges ruled, that there was a famine in the land. And a certain man of Bethlehem-Judah went to sojourn in the country of Moab, he, and his wife, and his two sons. And the name of the man was Elimelech, and the name of his wife Naomi, and the name of his two sons Mahlon and Chilion, Ephrathites of Bethlehem-Judah. And they came into the country of Moab, and continued there. And Elimelech Naomi's husband died; and she was left, and her two sons. And they took them wives of the women of Moab; the name of the one was Orpah, and the name of the other Ruth: and they dwelled there about ten years. And Mahlon and Chilion died also both of them; and the woman was left of her two sons and her husband."

Ruth 1:1-5

Life doesn't always turn out the way that we would like, and you can be assured there will be opportunities for hurts and disappointments to invade your life. Naomi's story is a prime example of how things can go wrong. She started out full, as she described herself, but ended up a widow. Not only was her husband dead, but so were her sons. What will she do, and how will she survive this traumatic loss? She now had only memories of her husband and sons. Naomi had lost all hope of ever having a full and happy life again. It was a difficult place to be. The grief of it weighed heavily on her. What do you do when life knocks you down, and it seems as if you cannot get back up? You must trust God to help you.' "Behold, I am the Lord, the God of all flesh: is there any thing too hard for me?" (Jeremiah 32:27). I submit to you, there is nothing too hard for God! "Behold, the Lord's hand is not shortened, that it cannot save; neither his ear heavy, that it cannot hear," (Isaiah 59:1).

A New Beginning for Naomi and Ruth

The storms of life will come, but the Lord's arms are always open to help you through them. You do not have to let negative situations keep you down. The Lord will help you to get back up again if you will let Him.

Elimelech had taken his family to Moab because of the famine in Israel. During this difficult time, Elimelech died. Can you imagine how hard this must have been for Naomi? She was already separated from her family and friends. She was living in a pagan country where her neighbors worshipped idol gods that were foreign to her. She knew that she needed her God. The One she could depend on to always make a way for her. She knew that these pagan gods could not help her. They were powerless! She longed for the God of Abraham, Isaac and Jacob. Although God was in her heart, she missed the assembling of other believers together to worship Him. Her sons, after some time, took wives of the women of Moab. Mahlon married Ruth and Chilion married Orpah. After they had lived there for around ten years, both, Mahlon and Chilion died. Naomi needed to draw strength from God to get through this intricate time.

After the death of her sons, Naomi made a conscious decision to leave Moab to return to Judah. She had heard that God had visited the people there and once again had made provision for them to have food. She knew that her life in Moab had been anything but easy. In fact, I believe it had been a very lonely life for Naomi. She was not a Christian because Jesus had not yet gone to the cross, but she was a believer.

Naomi so missed home. This was true of its physical location, but more importantly, it was because this was where God dwelled with His people. Nothing can compare to being in God's presence.

When I think about Christians today, it is daunting to see how many have become so preoccupied with the things of this world that they find themselves in a similar situation as Naomi. Not that they necessarily uproot their families and move to pagan countries, but rather they invest so much time in the things of this world that they spend virtually little to no time with the Lord. He wants us to enjoy a daily fellowship with Him and to be totally dependent upon Him. Quality and quantity of time with our Lord is essential! Romans 12:2 warns us about conforming to this world. If you find that you have fallen short in this area, my prayer is that you will repent and reconnect with the Lord Jesus. You cannot have a closer Friend—" and there is a friend that sticketh closer than a brother," (Proverbs 18:24).

It is imperative that you make time for God. After all, He is the One who created you, and surely, He knows what is best for you.

Naomi was now about to leave for Judah, but not without first stopping off to see her daughters-in-law, Orpah and Ruth. Naomi appreciated all that they had done for her and her sons. She sincerely loved them, but she knew that it was time to say good-bye and go back home. She had been gone much too long! What about you? True, this was about a geographical location, but I believe it could also be looked at in a symbolic way of your relationship with the Lord Jesus. Have you strayed away from Him? If so, isn't it time for you to return home? He loves you and is waiting for you to come back home.

As Naomi attempted to leave her daughters-in-law, I believe tears were shed and hugs and kisses were exchanged, but the young ladies were not willing to be separated from Naomi.

They wanted to go with her. Naomi insisted that they go back to their families. She knew she had no more sons and she wanted them to find love again with new husbands. After much conversing and weeping, Orpah turned back, but Ruth refused, and would not leave the woman that she had come to love.

A Made-up Mind

Ruth was determined that nothing Naomi said or did would stop her from going with her. She was willing to do whatever was necessary to remain with her mother-in-law and would not take , "no", for an answer.

"And Ruth said, Intreat me not to leave thee, or to return from following after thee: for whither thou goest, I will go, and where thou lodgest, I will lodge: thy people shall be my people, and thy God my God: Where thou diest, will I die, and there will I be buried: the LORD do so to me, and more also, if ought but death part thee and me. "

Ruth 1:16-17

Finally, Naomi gave in and allowed Ruth to come with her. What gave Ruth such a strong determination to go with her mother-in-law? It was obvious that she had a deep love for her mother-in-law. Perhaps, she remembered the happier times when Naomi would tell Ruth about her God, and all that He had done for the Israelites over the years. No doubt Ruth hid these truths deep within her heart, and only dreamed of having a God like this. Perhaps Ruth remembered the times when Naomi was so full of vitality and Ruth knew that she would not have this kind of life in her present state.

How wonderful it is to have someone in your life who will stick with you through the good times and the bad times. Ruth was indeed a true friend. Naomi must have felt all kinds of emotions as she and Ruth started the journey to her home town.

"So they went until they came to Bethlehem, and it came to pass, when they were come to Bethlehem, that all the city was moved about them, and they said, Is this Naomi? And she said unto them, Call me not Naomi, call me Mara; for the Almighty hath dealt very bitterly with me. I went out full, and the LORD hath brought me home again empty: why then call ye me Naomi, seeing the LORD hath testified against me, and the Almighty hath a licted me?"

Ruth 1:19-21 KJV

Naomi probably felt ashamed and guilty that she had lost everything, with the exception of Ruth. You know Satan must have spoken all kind of lies to her mind that she would be miserable for the rest of her life. When the town people saw her as she was returning home, they called her by Naomi, which meant pleasant, but she insisted that they call her Mara, which meant bitter. She saw her life as anything but pleasant . Beloved, you should never allow bad breaks to define you. You can rise above your circumstance with God' s help. The enemy will work overtime to make you feel useless and unimportant. Don' t believe his lies! No matter what mistakes you might have made, or how insignificant you may feel, God does not turn His back on you. Surely, there are consequences for our actions, but He loves us beyond our faults. You must trust Him, especially during the hard times. Run to Him, not from Him. God is a good God. He freely gives us choices, and when we make the wrong one , there are repercussions, but God will not give up on us and don' t you give up on Him! He is bigger than any problem that we will ever encounter.

Naomi seemed to have blamed God for what went wrong with her family. I am sure that deep within she knew to relocate to Moab was not His best for her family, but He honored Elimelech's and Naomi's decision. People usually look for someone to blame when misfortune occurs. They tend not to want to take responsibility for their own actions. Naomi, however, never gave up on the Lord, and it is certain that He never gave up on her. I have heard it said, and I concur, God does not make us bitter—He makes us better!

God can turn your negative situation around and cause it to work for your good—which is what He did in this story. I encourage you to read the Book of Ruth in its entirety to gain a better understanding of the Lord's marvelous love.

A Second Chance

When Naomi and Ruth arrived in Bethlehem, it was harvest time. Ruth ended up harvesting out of the field of Naom's rich relative, Boaz. God gave Ruth favor with Boaz. Naomi instructed Ruth on how to present herself to Boaz in hopes that he would marry Ruth and redeem the family inheritance. Boaz did just that! God blessed this couple with a son—Obed, whom Naomi helped to raise. Not only was Ruth blessed with a new husband and a son, but Naomi also had a new family. She was now full of joy! God had turned around what seemed like a hopeless situation into a fulfilled life. God gave Naomi and Ruth a second chance and a new beginning. He will do the same for you. Remember God loves you and wants to help you. Won't you let Him? Again, I remind you that this is an Old Testament story. We have a better covenant with God. We have Jesus interceding on our behalf!

Many times, we hear these words, "The best is yet to come." I have great news! His name is Jesus! And yes, He is coming back again! He promise that He would. (See John 14:1-3). Let us continue and see how Jesus has taken away our hurts with His precious blood. I trust that you will be encouraged.

Chapter Seven

Jesus: Our Savior, The Answer to All

We live in a fallen world that is full of trouble. It is without fail that the daily news carries stories of murders, robberies, rapes, shootings, and the list goes on and on. People are hurting. With so much turmoil, they wonder if peace will ever prevail again.

People are stressed and overwhelmed with simply trying to live their lives. They want to live happy and prosperous lives, but don't seem to know how to go about doing so. As a result, they find themselves leaning to their own understanding—which is not wise. Some may achieve financial success, but money alone will not bring about real peace or joy.

I have good news for the born-again believers! "Lift up your heads, O ye gates; even lift them up, ye everlasting doors, and the King of glory shall come in. Who is this King of glory? The LORD of hosts, He is the King of glory," (Psalm 24:9-10). Jesus is our peace. He has sent the Holy Spirit to take up residence on the inside of us, and He (the Holy Spirit) will lead and guide us into all truth.

"Howbeit when he, the Spirit of truth, is come, he will guide you into all truth: for he shall not speak of himself; but whatsoever he shall hear, that shall he speak: and he will shew you things to come."

John 16:13

"But the Comforter, which is the Holy Ghost, whom the Father will send in my name, he shall teach you all things,

and bring all things to your remembrance, whatsoever I have said unto you."

John 14:26

My sisters and brothers, whatever God has promised in His Word, He is able to perform. We do not have to live in fear, dread, or defeat. The Lord, through His grace and mercy, has made a way of escape. Jesus is our burden bearer. Jesus is to us whatever we need Him to be. Without Jesus, we would have no hope. Without Jesus, we would have no peace. Without Jesus, we would have no Savior, and without Jesus, we would be lost and hell bound. "Neither is there salvation in any other: for there is none other name under heaven given among men, whereby we must be saved," (Acts 4:12).

"For God so loved the world, that he gave his only begotten Son, that whosoever believeth in him should not perish, but have everlasting life," (John 3:16). God's love for mankind is far beyond our ability to comprehend. Jesus is the Answer to all of the turmoil that is going on in this world. Thank God for Jesus!

Man's Fall

We know the story of Adam and Eve and the perfect life they lived in the Garden of Eden before they blew it. They lived in an earthly paradise and everything that they needed was provided. They had eternal life, which meant that they were never to die. They were never to grow old. They were never to experience sin, sickness, disease, death, poverty, and the like. Life was awesome! The glory of God clothed them. The temperature was just right. The atmosphere was perfect. Every thing was perfect! God would walk through the garden in the cool of the day just to fellowship with them. Who could ask for anything more?

"And the LORD God took the man, and put him into the garden of Eden to dress it and to keep it. And the LORD God commanded the man, saying, Of every tree of the garden thou mayest freely eat: But of the tree of the knowledge of good and evil, thou shalt not eat of it: for in the day that thou eatest thereof thou shalt surely die." Eating of the forbidden fruit *shows they no longer trusted God to meet their needs, instead they trusted in themselves.*

Genesis 2:15-17

You would have thought that Adam would have gladly obeyed God's instructions, but we know the rest of the story, and it was not pretty. Eve allowed herself to be deceived by Satan and did eat of the fruit and gave it to her husband, Adam, and he also ate (Genesis 3:6). From that very moment, sin entered into the earth's realm, and Adam and Eve became separated from God and would experience death.

Even though this couple failed miserably in the garden, God's love for them never changed. He could not; however, allow them to remain in the garden. He had to remove them for their own protection, and for ours.

"And the LORD God said, Behold, the man is become as one of us, to know good and evil: and now, lest he put forth his hand, and take also of the tree of life, and eat, and live forever: Therefore the LORD God sent him forth from the garden of Eden, to till the ground from whence he was taken. So he drove out the man; and he placed at the east of the garden of Eden Cherubims, and a flaming sword which turned every way, to keep the way of the tree of life."

Genesis 3:22-24

It was never God's plan for mankind to know good and evil but because of Adam's and Eve's disobedience, they would know sin as would the entire human race.

"Unto the woman he said, I will greatly multiply thy sorrow and thy conception; in sorrow thou shalt bring forth children; and thy desire shall be to thy husband, and he shall rule over thee. And unto Adam he said, Because thou hast hearkened unto the voice of thy wife, and hast eaten of the tree, of which I commanded thee, saying, Thou shalt not eat of it: cursed is the ground for thy sake; in sorrow shalt thou eat of it all the days of thy life; Thorns also and thistles shall it bring forth to thee; and thou shalt eat the herb of the field; In the sweat of thy face shalt thou eat bread, till thou return unto the ground; for out of it wast thou taken: for dust thou art, and unto dust shalt thou return."

Genesis 3:16-19

"The old serpent, God cursed and he would crawl on his belly for the rest of his life and eat the dirt of the ground."

Genesis 3:14

When Adam violated God's command, the entire human race fell and was separated from God. Life as Adam and Eve knew had come to an end. This was not God's will; their disobedience cost them everything!

God's Strategic Plan to Redeem Mankind

God missed the fellowship that He had with Adam and Eve, and He wanted His family back. The Scripture let us know that God is a Holy God, and He cannot look upon sin (Habakkuk 1:13). Adam and Eve, because of their sinful act, were now separated from God, and thus, out of fellowship with Him. God knew that the only way that the human race could ever be redeemed was to provide a perfect sacrifice to satisfy the penalty of sin. No human qualified. "For all have sinned and come short of the glory of God," (Romans 3:23), but God, in His infinite wisdom, prepared a body for Jesus to enter into the earth by way of a virgin birth. Jesus was God in the flesh. "For the Son of man is come to save that which was lost," (Matthew 18:11). He taught and preached the Word of God (Matthew 4:17). "How God anointed Jesus of Nazareth with the Holy Ghost and with power: who went about doing good, and healing all that were oppressed of the devil; for God was with him," (Acts 10:38).

Jesus never lost focus of His mission. The religious crowd, however, found fault with His teachings and sought to take His life. Jesus said in John 10:18, "No man taketh it from me, but I lay it down of myself. I have power to lay it down, and I have power to take it again! This commandment have I received of my Father." Jesus says in John 10:30, "I and my Father are one." No man could take Jesus' life without His consent. He endured the cross for our sake. "As many were astonied at thee; his visage was so marred more than any man, and his form more than the sons of men," (Isaiah 52:14). Jesus was beaten so badly that His appearance was unrecognizable. "And the men that held Jesus mocked him, and smote him, And when they had blind folded him, they struck him on the face, and asked him, saying, Prophesy, who is it that smote thee? And many other things blasphemously spake they against him," (Luke 22:63 65). "And Jesus cried with a loud voice, and gave up the ghost," (Mark 15:37). After His horrific death.

He was buried in a tomb where He stayed for three days and three nights. He went to hell and took the keys from Satan. God raised Jesus from the dead on the third day with all power in His hands. "I am he that liveth, and was dead; and, be hold, I am alive for evermore, Amen; and have the keys of hell and of death," (Revelation 1:18). "And Jesus came and spake unto them, saying. All power is given unto me in heaven and in earth," (Matthew 28:18). Jesus walked the earth for forty days before He ascended to Heaven. "Looking unto Jesus the author and finisher of our faith; who for the joy that was set before him endured the cross, despising the shame, and is set down at the right hand of the throne of God," (Hebrews 12:2).

Jesus is still interceding on our behalf. We no longer have to let our ouches, hurts, and disappointments stop us! We may still feel them, but don't despair. We have been empowered by Almighty God, through Jesus to be victorious. I encourage you to use your authority and to speak God's Word over your life and see the salvation of the Lord.

My friend, Jesus is coming back for His born-again believers— "...Ye men of Galilee, why stand ye gazing up into heaven? This same Jesus, which is taken up from you into heaven, shall so come in like manner as ye have seen him go into heaven," (Acts 1:11). "And if I go and prepare a place for you, I will come again, and receive you unto myself; that where I am, there ye may be also," (John 14:3).

Salvation is More Than Keeping Us Out of Hell!

Jesus' victory far transcends just keeping us out of hell! As awesome as that is, and thank God that born-again believers won't experience hell, but Jesus has equipped us to live abundant lives right now. Here are some Scriptures that I hope will encourage you:

"Then Peter began to say unto him, Lo, we have left all, and have followed thee. And Jesus answered and said, Verily I say unto you, There is no man that hath left house, or brethren, or sisters, or father, or mother, or wife, or children, or lands, for my sake, and the gospel's. But he shall receive an hundredfold now in this time, houses, and brethren, and sisters, and mothers, and children, and lands, with persecutions; and in the world to come eternal life."

Mark 10: 28-30

"The thief cometh not, but for to steal, and to kill, and to destroy: I am come that they might have life, and that they might have it more abundantly. "

John 10:10

Jesus wants us to enjoy our lives. He says in Luke 12:32, *"Fear not, little flock; for it is your Father's good pleasure to give you the kingdom."*

Faith is Essential for Salvation

Jesus has already provided salvation for all who will believe and receive by grace through faith, His finished work at the cross. Titus 2:11 says, "For the grace of God that bringeth salvation hath appeared to all men. "Does this mean that all people will be saved? No! Only those who by grace, through faith, believe and receive the finished work of Jesus. "But without faith it is impossible to please Him; for he that cometh to God must believe that he is, and that he is a rewarder of them that diligently seek him, " (Hebrews 11:6)

"For by grace are ye saved through faith; and that not of yourselves: it is the gift of God: Not of works, lest any man should boast. For we are his workmanship, created in Christ Jesus unto good works, which God hath before ordained that we should walk in them."

Ephesians 2:8-10

The Greek word for salvation according to the *Vines Complete Expository Dictionary* is soteria which denotes: deliverance, preservation, salvation, safety, and health. 1 Vine, W.E, Merrill F. Unger, and William White. Vine's Complete Expository, Dictionary of Old and New Testament Words, 1984.

Mankind-Tripartite

We are created in the image and likeness of God (Genesis 1:26-27). He is God the Father, God the Son, and God the Holy Spirit— The Trinity, or the Triune God, three distinct persons in One.

We are a spirit. This is the part of us that is born-again when we accept Jesus' finished work at the cross. We possess a soul, which comprises of our mind, will, emotions and intellect, and we live in a physical or natural body. "And the very God of peace sanctify you wholly; and I pray God your whole spirit and soul and body be preserved blameless unto the coming of our Lord Jesus Christ," (1 Thessalonians 5:23). When we become born-again, we become new creatures with new natures. "Therefore if any man be in Christ, he is a new creature: old things are passed away; behold, all things are become new," (2 Corinthians 5:17). As previously stated, it is our spirit-man that gets born-again. As we begin the process of renewing our minds with the Word of God, we will see changes in our behavior.

"And be not conformed to this world: but be ye transformed by the renewing of your mind, that ye may prove what is that good, and acceptable, and perfect, will of God," (Romans 12: 2). The key to our born- again experience is that we must believe by faith in the finished work of Jesus. It is more than just having head knowledge of Him. It is a heart transformation. Jesus must become our Lord and Savior. " Finally, my brethren, be strong in the Lord, and in the power of his might," (Ephesians 6:10).

We can fellowship with Jesus at any time. He is never too busy to spend time with us. In fact, the Lord looks forward to our time together. It pleases Him. "But thou art holy, O thou that inhabitest the praises of Israel," (Psalms 22:3). Not only does He inhabit the praises of Israel, but He inhabits the praises of His people everywhere.

God Loads Us with Benefits Daily

By virtue of being born-again, we enjoy many of God's daily blessings. "And if ye be Christ's, then are ye Abraham's seed, and heirs according to the promise," (Galatians 3:29). Romans 8:17 states, "And if children, then heirs; heirs of God, and joint-heirs with Christ...." God wants to lavish His children daily with blessings, but some are not mature enough to receive God' s blessing. They may have to wait for a while, but the Lord is longsuffering, and won't forget them. Our blessings should never be more important to us than He who provides the blessings. Of course, our greatest desire should always be to fellowship with the Lord because we want to, and not just for benefits. Here are some benefits that Jesus has made available to us. We must receive them by placing faith in Him.

"BLESS the LORD, O my soul: and all that is within me, bless his holy name. Bless the LORD, O my soul, and forget not all his benefits: Who forgiveth all thine iniquities; who healeth all thy diseases; Who redeemeth thy life from destruction; who crowneth thee with lovingkindness and tender mercies; Who satisfieth thy mouth with good things, so that thy youth is renewed like the eagle's."

Psalms 103:1-5

"Blessed be the Lord, who daily loadeth us with benefits, even the God of our salvation."

Psalm 68:19

"Blessed be the God and Father of our Lord Jesus Christ, who hath blessed us with all spiritual blessings in heavenly places in Christ," (Ephesians 1:3). This means that we are already blessed through Christ Jesus. We show our gratitude through praising the Lord, worshipping Him and resting in His finished work.

"Having predestinated us unto the adoption of children by Jesus Christ to himself, according to the good pleasure of his will," (Ephesians 1:5), we have been adopted into the family of God. We are no longer outcasts, but we have been granted entrance into the very presence of God through Jesus Christ. We are of His household! My sisters and brothers, we are joint-heirs with Jesus Christ (Romans 8:17). Let that resonate in your heart!

"To the praise of the glory of his grace, Wherein He hath made us accepted in the beloved," (Ephesians 1:6). We don't have to wonder if we are acceptable to God or if He is pleased with us. This scripture plainly tells us that we are acceptable to Him through what Jesus had done for us. It was our spirit that was made perfect. "Know ye not that ye are the temple of God, and that the Spirit of God dwelleth in you?" (1 Corinthians 3:16). "In whom ye also trusted, after that ye heard the word of truth, the gospel of your salvation: in whom also after that ye believed, ye were sealed with that Holy Spirit of promise," (Ephesians 1:13). Our spirit-man is perfect. Jesus paid the price for it.

"In whom we have redemption through his blood, the forgiveness of sins, according to the riches of his grace," (Ephesians 1:7). We have been delivered from sin. We have been set free through the shed blood of Jesus on the cross. "If the Son therefore shall make you free, ye shall be free indeed," (John 8:36). We have forgiveness of all of our sins. How can we not love Jesus? No one else could do for us what Jesus has done. Hallelujah to His Holy name!

Beloved, Jesus is the One who has taken our ouches and hurts upon Himself. Jesus bore our grief and carried our sorrows (Isaiah 53:4). We are to cast our cares upon Him because He cares for us (1 Peter 5:7). Jesus said that He would perfect all that concerns us (Psalms 138:8). My brothers and sisters, He has done it all! When the enemy tries to discourage you and you find yourself headed for another pity party, Stop! I encourage you to open your mouth and shout out loud, "I am the righteousness of God in Christ Jesus," (2 Corinthians 5:21), "Christ in me is the hope of glory!" (Colossians 1:27), and "Jesus has borne my hurts. I will not be robbed of my destiny!"

A Better Covenant

The Old Testament believers had God working on their behalf, and Satan could not destroy them because God was with them.

My friend, born-again believers have a much better covenant. Jesus has provided it. "But now hath he obtained a more excellent ministry, by how much also he is the mediator of a better covenant, which was established upon better promises," (Hebrews 8:6).

I encourage you to research the covenants and study them for your own spiritual growth. This book does not provide a study of the covenants, but only provides some scriptural references.

Under the old covenant, unblemished animals, such as bullocks and goats, were brought to the high priest to be offered to God as sacrifices for the atonement of sins for the people, as well as for the priest himself. The blood of these animals could not remove sins, but only covered them for one year at a time (Exodus and Numbers). In the new covenant, Jesus' precious blood that was shed at the cross took away all of our sins—past, present and future—so that we might be made the righteousness of God in Christ Jesus! (2 Corinthians 5:21, 1 John 2:2, and Hebrews 9). Jesus made the ultimate sacrifice, and there will never be a need for another sin offering. His precious blood has provided redemption. Death could not hold Him, He rose from the grave on the third day with all power in His hands. Because He lives, we live!

We are no longer under the law of the Old Testament, but we are now under grace because of Jesus' finished work at the cross.

Does this mean because we are under grace that we continue in sin? The answer is a resounding NO! This question was asked to the Apostle Paul and here is his response: "WHAT shall we say then? Shall we continue in sin, that grace may abound? God forbid. How shall we, that are dead to sin, live any longer therein?" (Romans 6:1-2). When we understand the love of God—as much as our finite minds can, why would anyone want to continue in sin? God HATES sin and so should we.

Here are some uplifting Scriptures to meditate:

I John 4:4

"Ye are of God, little children, and have overcome them: because greater is he that is in you, than he that is in the world."

3 John 1:2

"Beloved, I wish above all things that thou mayest prosper and be in health, even as thy soul prospereth."

1 Peter 2:24

"Who his own self bare our sins in his own body on the tree that we being dead to sins, should live unto righteousness; by whose stripes ye were healed."

Romans 8:37

"Nay, in all these things we are more than conquerors through him that loved us."

ROMANS 8:11

"But if the Spirit of him that raised up Jesus from the dead dwell in you, he that raised up Christ from the dead shall also quicken your mortal bodies by his Spirit that dwelleth in you."

John 10:27

"My sheep hear my voice, and I know them, and they follow me,"

John 10:28

"And I give unto them eternal life; and they shall never perish, neither shall any man pluck them out of my hand."

John 10:29

"My Father, which gave them me, is greater than all; and no man is able to pluck them out of my Father's hand."

John 3:16

For God so loved the world that He gave His only begotten Son that whosoever believeth in Him should not perish, but have everlasting life.

Romans 8:1

"There is therefore now no condemnation to them which are in Christ Jesus, who walk not after the flesh, but after the Spirit."

I will conclude this book with these powerful words of encouragement:

If God Be for Us, Who Can Be Against Us?

Romans 8:31-35, 37-39

"What shall we then say to these things? If God be for us, who can be against us? He that spared not his own Son, but delivered him up for us all, how shall he not with him also freely give us all things? Who shall lay anything to the charge of God's elect? It is God that justifieth. Who is he that condemneth? It is Christ that died, yea rather, that is risen again, who is even at the right hand of God, who also maketh intercession for us. Who shall separate us from the love of Christ? shall tribulation, or distress, or persecution, or famine, or nakedness, or peril, or sword? ... Nay, in all these things we are more than conquerors through him that loved us. For I am persuaded, that neither death, nor life nor angels, nor principalities, nor powers, nor things present, nor things to come, Nor height, nor depth, nor any other creature, shall be able to separate us from the love of God, which is in Christ Jesus our Lord."

"Dear Reader," Jesus loves you! He is indeed the answer to all of your problems. You need not hold your head down any longer. Instead, hold your head up high. Jesus has already defeated Satan! Believe and receive the blessings that He has for you. Remember, you are blessed above all people (Deuteronomy 7:14), and you are highly favored (Luke 1:28). For God so loved the world that He gave His only begotten Son that whosoever believeth in Him should not perish, but have everlasting life.

Prayer Guide for Salvation

If you don't know Jesus, why not make Him your personal Savior and Lord right now? He is cheering for you, and oh, how He will encourage you. When no one else is around, Jesus will be there for you. By faith, receive this precious Gift, and all the benefits that comes with this relationship.

> *"But what saith it? The Word is nigh thee, even in thy mouth, and in thy heart: that is, the word of faith which we preach: That if thou shalt confess with thy mouth the Lord Jesus, and shalt believe in thine heart that God hath raised him from the dead, thou shalt be saved. For with the heart man believeth unto righteousness; and with the mouth confession is made unto salvation,"*

Romans 10:8-10

In Romans 10:13, we find these words, "For whosoever shall call upon the name of the Lord shall be saved. " Please pray this prayer if you are sincere in making Jesus your Lord and Savior:

Lord Jesus, I believe you are the Son of God—that You died for my sins on the cross, and God raised You from the dead. I repent of my sins and I confess that You are my Lord and Savior. By faith in Your Word Lord Jesus, I receive You now. Thank You for loving me, saving me, and giving me eternal life. I am now a child of the most high God, and Heaven is my home. Amen.

I believe if you prayed in sincerity, you are born-again. If you were out of the will of God and were sincere with your prayer you have been restored to the family of God. "For sin shall not have dominion over you: for you are not under law, but under grace," (Romans 6:14). Here is the good news, God has delivered you from the power of darkness and translated you into the kingdom of His dear Son, Jesus! (Colossians 1:13).

Congratulations! You have just made the best decision of your life! Now, find a church to attend on a regular basis that teaches and preaches the Word of God to foster your spiritual growth.

Renewing of the Mind

Now that you have made Jesus your Lord and Savior, it is crucial that you begin the process to renew your mind.

"I BESEECH you therefore, brethren, by the mercies of God, that ye present your bodies a living sacrifice, holy, acceptable unto God, which is your reasonable service. And be not conformed to this world: but be ye transformed by the renewing of your mind, that ye may prove what is that good, and acceptable, and perfect, will of God."

Romans 12:1-2

Renewing of the mind is a daily process. I encourage you to read, study and meditate on God's Word, and it will begin to transform your life.

About the Author

Rosa L. Booker resides in Buckingham County, Virginia. She has one sister, Janie F. Booker and two brothers, Deacon Bernard Booker (Sheila), Rev. Calvin H. Booker, Sr. (Joyce). Rosa believes the Holy Spirit inspired her to write this book to encourage Christians to remain steadfast in faith and not to lose hope—no matter what might be going on in this world. God's Word has not changed—nor can it! He is the same yesterday, today and forever. Our future is bright! We have challenges, but we don't quit. We go through them with God's grace and mercy.

Minister Rosa is grateful to God for having chosen her to write this book. She has been in ministry for over twenty years and loves teaching and preaching the Word of God. Much of her ministry has been in Outreach. Currently Rosa serves as the Assistant Pastor of the Petersville Baptist Church in Buckingham County under the leadership of Pastor Ollie W. Bolden and Co-Pastor Cynthia Bolden.